Positive & Negative Christianity:
A Perspective on the Law of Attraction Theory

S. Margot Schultz

M.A., M.T.S., NCC

ISBN:1481071947
ISBN-13: 978-1481071949

DEDICATION

To my loving family members who care each and every day: Bestamor, John, and Briavel (who will be a writer). Thank you, thank you, and thank you.

To all the book groups and Bible studies I have ever been in, thank you for going on the Journey with me.

To all the mentors, professors, and ministers who have ever shared their knowledge with me: I took courage from your example.

To the Schultz family for their loyalty and financial support through the many lean years of graduate school, I can only stand in awe of the miracles.

CONTENTS

ACKNOWLEDGMENTS

This book came about as I attempted to solve a problem that the Law of Attraction theory, a subset of Positive Psychology, presents to the system of Christian Theology in general.

1   INTRODUCTION

The theory of Positive Psychology has wide appeal in our chaotic world. Many books have been written about this research. Martin Seligman made very good use of this (1990/1998, *Learned Optimism*) when studying political campaigns. He said, in essence, that the candidate with the most optimism wins. In his research, he sorted through the statements and beliefs coming from campaign speeches and interviews given by the candidates. Naturally there is a wide variety during any given election. His filter was to search for who sounded the most optimistic. Seligman was convinced that audiences were listening for which candidate could persuade them to feel good, or at least better, about the future.

A second layer to this optimism literature, found in the realm of inspirational books, is called Law of Attraction theory. It has taken the idea of "appealing" to a whole new level. It starts with the same basic tenets of positive thinking, adds in business success principles, and coaches us toward feeling better. In addition, Law of Attraction theory (LOA) asserts that feelings in and of themselves are magnets, a physical force. This combination of psychology and physics puts LOA in the category of Metaphysics but it is not written in that style. It is written usually as a "how to" manual. In other words, LOA writers will have you practice, just as a coach would. First, you practice thinking positive thoughts specific to your situation, just as you would "reframe" with a counselor or a psychologist. Over time, these would help you begin to germinate and grow positive feelings. Then, with enough practice, LOA writers will have you jumping straight to the positive feelings as needed in order to keep your day and your energy flowing well and at such a high level that events and people will align in cooperation with your best intentions. To quote a best-seller in this genre: "Focus on what we want with passion and excitement, and presto! It's on its way!" (Grabhorn, 2000).

Even if the underlying principle of optimism might be operating, this kind of seductive language is an affront to our reality-testing adult minds. What are we supposed to do with such magical thinking!? This is the problem which the Law of Attraction poses. The reason we even spend any time considering this principle is because the science of psychology research has shown us that deliberate thinking of positive thoughts and positive interpretations of events does indeed help us feel better over the long run. But the trick is, we have to sneak around our own natural tendency to let the "inner critic" dominate. No one wants to play the fool or be called ridiculous.

In Christian thought, there is general agreement that God is benevolent, and therefore, allowing for a few nasty exceptions, God's universe is set up to allow each one of us a chance for freedom to construct a life of moderate contentment. The scholars can give you many interpretations of a scripture verse such as "God is able to provide you with every blessing in abundance so that by always having enough of everything, you may share abundantly in every good work." (2 Cor.9:8) This passage indicates the Christian worldview that God wants good gifts for each person. It is "top-down." The LOA is even broader than this. It holds that anyone who can just generate enough good feelings will tap into an infinite power source. It is more egalitarian or "side-to-side" in that permission does not have to be granted by God for the blessings to flow. In LOA, the view of the universe is more mechanistic, somewhat like the need to generate electricity because life in the Arctic Circle can't be normal without heat for the houses.

A Christian Positive Psychology would include a living God directing the flow of energy. It implies a relationship between people and God, such as we find discussed in the Old Testament book of Chronicles (1 Chron. 22:13), "Then you will prosper if you are careful to observe the statutes and the ordinances that the Lord commanded Moses for Israel. Be strong and of good courage. Do not be afraid or dismayed." It is **not** saying that the greedy do not prosper, but rather, that once a person is a follower of the most holy God, divine assistance flows within these boundaries or ethical expectations, if you will. In contrast to prosperity, both the Jewish and the Christian traditions have much to say about the rapidly shifting fortunes of evil-doers. What goes up can always come down. They want to say that there is no safety net for the unethically ambitious ones of this world. LOA is strangely silent on this point, except to point out how hard it is for devious people to stay out of negative vibrational patterns (which is the kiss of death in LOA).

The Law of Attraction writers will argue that, if your fortunes come crashing down, it is your *own fault*, i.e. for dwelling on bad feelings or worries about worst-case scenarios. LOA's "look the other way" posture toward misfortune appears to be almost superstitious. Doesn't it seem odd to be afraid of your own strong opinions against what is going wrong in your life? Yet this is exactly what LOA writers will harp on. In contrast, a faith-based perspective on failures and foibles does not set out to blame the victim! You are allowed to feel your emotions without fear of repercussions. If there is a backlash to feeling angry, it is not because God wants to punish the disenchanted ones among us. No, the backlash is from how stubborn of a state anger is. It doesn't want to let you go, once you are "in the door." It takes a mature and cunning person to stay out of the clutches of negativity.

LOA's favorite point about "watching which feeling-state you are in" is an excellent observation to make several times a day about yourself. Bravo to the LOA theory for stimulating this awareness in each of us. It is good psychological practice to gently nudge our own thoughts and feelings toward a positive re-framing. You never know when you are going to need to draw upon the emotional bank account of good feelings in a pinch of difficulty. As we all know, the modern world is not set up to be cozy and cuddly. You and I may walk around spreading good feelings as much as we want, but the institutions that govern us (work, school, government, banks, service providers, utilities, etc.) are quite capable of dumping their chaos in our laps. Then what? Each of us has a choice whether to be dragged into pessimism by such experiences.

Speaking of chaos, another reason why LOA cannot substitute well for a faith-based worldview is that it cannot separate out good from evil. To equate anything and everything that happens with the mysterious force field of energy surrounding each person is ridiculous! This author cannot imagine telling a soldier that the reason his arm was blown off was because he was thinking negative thoughts about his enemy. War is evil and placing oneself into armed conflict will open up opportunity for serious injury to occur. People in battle think thoughts of annihilating each other because that is the social agreement between opposing sides. The only question is: do you want to participate? If you are a follower of LOA theory, then you would probably answer 'no' to involving yourself in all those negative thoughts. This is actually very wise, but it doesn't explain evil. Evil is the seduction of believing that you will become a hero if you go into battle. It includes the narcissism of assuming that you won't be hurt because you are more skilled than the other fighters, or perhaps more protected in your specialness. Men and women go in to war all the time in order to test this belief about themselves. This brings us to the problem of God on the battlefield.

C.S. Lewis rightly pointed out that "the everythingist, if he starts from God, becomes a pantheist; there must be nothing that is not God." LOA is a theory of Everything. Everywhere you look, you can claim that the Law of Attraction is at work. Blame any problem on the fact that a person was not keeping their energy at the right level. This actually helps those of us who are studying religious faith because we learn not to make this mistake of pantheism that LOA so beautifully illustrates for us. What do I mean? All the events that happen on a battlefield are not God's doing. We know from looking at hundreds of scriptural passages and scholarly interpretations of those passages that, by and large, God wants peace and health for the people of this world. If war can be avoided: wonderful. If war can be shortened or lessened, it is the enlightened choice. But when so much disobedience and sin build up into powder-keg of conflict, then the explosion will just have to occur to release the pressure. It doesn't mean that God likes conflagration. It means humans have not learned to de-escalate in a timely way. To complete the point of C.S. Lewis, "All things are related in different and complicated ways. But all things are not One." (Miracles, 1947/1974).

To say more about evil before we leave this topic: isn't it strange the way LOA writers discuss negative thoughts like proverbial snakes moving about in the garden of Eden, stirring up trouble for each one of us? There are just too many types of thoughts and feelings in any one day to worry about each one. One stray negative thought is not going to come back to ambush you in two weeks! It is the general tone of internal dialogue that creates your moods over a given week or two weeks. One would hope not to get into the habit of obsessing about cleaning and tidying *all* feelings, just to please the almighty LOA rules. It is not healthy nor helpful to live in fear of contamination from "emotional garbage" clogging the planet.

2 WHAT THE L.O.A. DOES RIGHT

What we notice first is that the LOA writers are very careful to distinguish envy from visualizing abundance. When working with images of a positive scene about one's own very bright future, it is important to stay on the side of joy, rather than stray over into feelings of lack. A focus on "not enough" of something will indeed put you into a bad mood; however LOA theory would have you believe that merely spending a few minutes in this state will pull deficits (lack) right into your future in the next few months. The same pity is given to poor souls who spend any time in a state of jealousy, which is also considered a focus on lack but with the added layer of comparing this to someone who has more. What is a person to do instead? Aren't we free beings who can think whatever we want, whenever we want to think about it?!

Here is where Mindfulness technique has already paved the way for us. Any who have read or been taught Mindfulness recall that "savoring the moment" is a focus on what is satisfying or beautiful in that place where you are, doing what you are doing with relish. You enhance your own experience on purpose because this releases good feelings that are waiting to come forth. The same is true for LOA theory: spend time imagining how you want a situation to look, or turn out, then borrow those feelings as if it is actually happening. The trick is not to think about how this scene has not happened yet. Just like Mindfulness, the more you learn to hold your attention on the goal, the closer you are to arriving at it. This is no different than sports psychology which is used to train athletes to visualize perfect performance many times a day, so that when the hour of competition arrives, the athletes are prepared to win in their mind and not just with their muscles.

Why the law of attraction needs to have energy vortexes as part of its rationale begs the question of which "Unseen Forces" are at work. Granted, this is a common-enough question, if we only just look at Freud and Jung and Psychodynamic theory. They asked: what is that sneaky Unconscious part of our brain up to? We want to know because we see people behaving in such odd ways. Or in Physics, what is that Higges-Boson particle doing that makes all the other particles behave that way? It turns out that LOA theory is heavily invested in combining psychology with physics. Once the brain is understood to be a quantum machine, the rest of the LOA paradigm falls into place. For more on the details of this aspect of the LOA model of the brain, see *The Science Behind The Secret* by Travis Taylor, Ph.D.

The LOA writers just want you to ask: "Why couldn't life be better than it is right now?" Using the imagination, plus a hundred little moments of opportunity, means that the situation could look completely different. Herein lies the creativity of LOA thinking. The more you ponder what you would like to see happen, the more "outside the box" connections you make in your mind as it tries to connect the dots between "here now" over to "there, as I would like it to be." Don't forget emotion; if you have enough emotion to be jealous of someone else's good fortune, then you have enough emotion to redirect your focus onto your own goals. The only problem that LOA writers don't solve is, what if a person has little or no emotion? Their whole technique rests on a person's capability to have lots of feelings.

LOA theory flies straight in the face of Realists, and it shows no shame in doing so. To prove this, just try explaining LOA to anyone who has lived through World War II or The Great Depression. They will tell you that there was no law of attraction around to help them during their suffering. The finesse of LOA is that it brings imagination and vision out of the realm of childhood memories and back into the adult world. And who let them in the door? Well, people like Napoleon Hill and Dale Carnegie did. The power of positive thinking has been hanging around the sales office of every corporation since the 1950's. How do you think the sales staff stands it, trying to drum up business out of thin air? They have to think big, think happy, and attract every last scrap of enthusiasm they can find. They have honed this technique to a fine point for us. It keeps them alive in the worst economic dry-spells.

If an athlete can win the Olympics and a politician can win an election just by thinking this way, why can't an ordinary citizen benefit from such methods? At first glance, it would seem this is purely a matter of taste. If a person can stomach this rich food of super-charged positivity then, of course, we would expect them to take it on with gusto. But what about the melancholy types who would recoil at this, even though they are the ones most in need of a tonic for what ails them? LOA teachings are trying to light a fire under the apathetic types, first by using desire, then imagination, then goal-setting. They are trying to give us some pointers about knowing ourselves right down to the texture and tone of what feelings are flowing through us.

3 RESPONSE TO THE LOA

The Christian worldview is all about attracting good outcomes. Prayer was invented for this very purpose, so LOA has no corner and no exclusive contract on this activity. Let us take the famous passage from Romans 8:28, "We know that God causes all things to work together for the good of those who love God and are called according to God's purpose for them." This contains an added layer of purpose over and above the intention of attracting positive outcomes. For a Christian, God wants to bestow more grace on each of us than what could possibly be "magnetically attracted" on our own. If you combine powerful prayers of positive outcomes with the boost that a loving God can give to a mere human, that is Attraction squared.

The second important difference is for the Christians reading this. Some followers of Jesus Christ walk around saying "I just have to accept the way things are. God has put me into this particular position in life to learn some lesson. My job is to be humble about it." This is neutralizing rhetoric and a way to keep peace with yourself. Peace is a good resting place. At some point, it will be time to make a move again. The motion is from acceptance to feeling a desire to make a change. This is where visualizing great abundance comes in handy. A person of faith would find inspiration in a passage such as Nehemiah 2:20, "I replied to them 'The God of heaven is the one who will give us success, and we God's servants are going to start building...'" Notice the self-confidence that the prophet has here! He has no doubt that God wants to send forth blessings upon their initiative.

When the God of the Old Testament promises abundance for those following the covenant, it does not sound like words of permissiveness. LOA theorists would have you believe that the greater your desire is, combined with your capacity to feel and visualize, then the greater your reward will be. Humans might *want* to hear that the universe is our Candy Store, yet is it the truth? Perhaps it was true in your childhood. LOA theory is standing up for the enthusiasm of your childhood. Getting these memories to persist and work for you in your time of need (for a good feeling) is the goal that LOA writers are after. Yet a Christian perspective is more focused on eternal time and the long view. "When I was a child, I talked like a child, I thought like a child, I reasoned like a child. When I became a man, I put childish ways behind me." (1 Cor. 13:11, NIV) Does this mean that Christians are too mature to bother with the LOA? The answer comes in the definition of what prayer is. In prayer we acknowledge our dependence on God, just like a child depends on a parent. Fear is kept at bay by the parent.

Prayer is different from the law of attraction teachings because one can have confidence that our loving God is fully able to receive our requests, cleanse the fear/negativity from them, and help us to move toward a better future, with better outcomes. Still it is interesting to note how many times messengers from God have told humans "be not afraid." It seems to be a consistent theme, whether it was listed in scripture 79 times or 46 times, or somewhere in between. A faith-based perspective is that fear can be acknowledged. An LOA perspective would be more extreme, warning us not to allow talk of fears at any time because this will attract bad occurrences or mishaps. Doesn't this sound rather like having a head cold, but pretending you have plenty of energy to go to work anyway? A little bit of denial can be called distraction by Positive Thinking, but constant denial just sets a person up for a back-lash of unacknowledged feelings. Even the supremely confident LOA writer L. Grabhorn admitted that after having many successful days of attracting what she wanted, there would come an unexplainable day of darkest depression. She could never figure out why.

Why rush past the subject of human sadness or fears, and only talk about happy memories from childhood or what we have always wanted from the Universal Candy Store? LOA makes the mistake of layering the sugar-coating of "Positive and Happy" over any and every kind of situation. The cake will not set up properly unless you get the ingredients right. Louise Hay, another LOA teacher, gets this point right when she advises readers to affirm such statements as "I release all grudges and slights from my past. I release all negative patterns and habits." (1990, Hay) She is acknowledging the shadow side of human emotions. A Christian would add one more ingredient, saying "I ask God for help releasing my anger, and for forgiveness for what I have done wrong, even if I didn't understand it at the time."

Let's give LOA the benefit of the doubt and suppose that the main point is to increase our positive-focus attention span. When praying, can we hold a positive image of our sick friend getting better and feeling well, for more than 16 seconds? Observe how quickly your mind flips out of trust-mode and slips away down the path of worrying about the friend? Notice the difference between saying: "My friend is so sick God. Please help him," and saying "Your healing Light is so powerful Lord God. Please pour forth your love over my friend in all ways: body, mind, and soul. May they receive your blessings today each hour and know the power of your Mercy." The first is like a stick-drawing with hardly any color. The second has image and color and thus pulls more emotion into the prayer. At the very least, it cannot hurt you to be more in touch with your emotions while praying. At best, this prayer is more heart-felt and earnest; closer to the John 15:7 ideal of "abiding" in God. This verse is a hint about what it takes to receive answers.

4 HOW GROUP PRAYER IMITATES MAGNETICS

Since the last chapter was about praying for others, we will look at how LOA theory agrees with observations that Christians have made about prayer. First, focusing on specific intentions for each member of a prayer group seems to heighten the effect, meaning more obvious results are noticed. After a few days or weeks, a participant will often explain how that particular prayer was answered. This is not only great for the one who was prayed for, but it also enhances the prayer group's belief that their intercessory prayer made a difference. Similarly, Attraction writers (LOA) will tell you that getting a corporate team into the "habit of expectation" will improve performance - such that more business actually does come in. The expectation is like an echo bouncing around the echo chamber. Each person is sending forward what they heard, as a reinforcer. The success-oriented thoughts and feelings have been magnified. So whether it is a prayer group feeling the excitement of answered prayer or an employee team at work, it helps tremendously to invoke the power of the group mind toward beneficial outcomes.

One thing that the LOA books do really well is to show us the simplicity of the following affirmation (or prayer, depending on your beliefs): "I am open to receive blessings." This phrase has many psychological benefits when it becomes a habit and an emotional posture toward life. Notice it does not use the word "want" which has a more self-oriented sound. The more individuals or prayer groups can say this, the higher likelihood of staying positive. Those of us who do pray (compared to practicing affirmations only) have to be careful how we pray because of all the sadness in the world – which gets sent straight to the prayer groups for intercession! Framing the prayers in the most open-handed, receptive, blessing-oriented way will keep us from "lock-down" into low moods while pondering the misfortunes of others.

So many people of faith are saying odd phrases like "God is pruning me." This is a reference to the parable of the Vine (John 15:2) which goes like this: "Every branch that bears fruit he [God] prunes to make it bear more fruit." This brings up a very intricate question to address. How long is difficulty supposed to last? The LOA would have you think that the duration of challenging times is totally up to you. It depends on how much negativity you put out there. In contrast, a religious perspective would first ponder the qualities of a person's character. What character-defect, or weakness, is surfacing during this time of difficulty? If there are no obvious lessons to be learned, then perhaps the struggle will be over soon. After all, it is no problem for a strong person to use their strength on any given day. Furthermore, a strong person would be using confidence to get through a struggle, just like the LOA theory recommends. Praying for the future to turn out well, visualizing a fountain of joy, feeling good feelings of trust, and imagining that all shall be well: these are what persons of faith have in common with LOA writings.

What works for you, that brings joy into your day? This writer feels joy in seeing others in love with God, enjoying getting along well with others. Also, it is heartening to find little indications that the extended family or community is stable and at peace. Even though the LOA writers talk about pulling material rewards towards oneself through "magnetics," this can only be *part* of a daily practice because it is not very satisfying to the soul. Let us agree to also use the power of group attraction to practice positive thoughts for our country; to visualize a wave of healing rippling from one shore to the other, touching all in its path with a return to a healthy society and "the way things need to be."

One of my favorite images of plenty from the Old Testament is that of King Solomon. The writers made no apologies about how perfect this icon's life was, right down to the last detail. To top it all off, he was remembered for being wise and virtuous so no one could say that he was shallow or had gotten his wealth through stealth or other unscrupulous means. He has been set before us as a model of a person who sought God's instruction and received guidance on everything, including how to become more wealthy. Just reading about Solomon will put you in the frame of mind to think prosperous thoughts from a lofty point of view. Speaking of lofty, Solomon got away with thinking well of himself for a very long time, until one day he forgot the very important principle of **loyalty**. In 1 Kings 11:8 we hear that he broke faith and offered incense to foreign deities. God Almighty (of the covenant) had been betrayed. The flow of blessings and closeness with God came to a halt. He was told that his kingdom would break apart during his son's lifetime.

Interestingly, he was also told that the faith of his father, David, would cover for some of his mistakes. It was as if the family's prayer-power had a long-lasting protective effect over his fate, so that he did not fail immediately, nor utterly.

5 DISTRACTION AND FLOW

Religious people know full well that there is energy in prayer. Feelings of heat, power, tingling or even tears accompany intense prayer. LOA "magnetics" theory is borrowing from this well-known phenomenon. The tricky part of a prayer life is in the "flow" of how and when prayers get answered. If a prayer is answered quickly, it is easy to keep the positive feelings going. But what if a petition for divine help takes weeks and weeks before results are manifested? Similarly, LOA writers will tell you that most complaints about their teachings come because "good things" are not happening fast enough for followers of their method. What is the prescription then? Actually, they have good suggestions! To span the time from the past to the future, it is recommended to borrow good feelings from what has already gone well, otherwise known as gratitude; then to project forward into how grateful you WILL BE when the hoped-for things come true.

When a person of faith is watching for little signs or indications from God that an answer is in the making, this is no different from LOA practitioners looking for synchronicity of events as proof that "the universe" is bringing about their wish. Yet isn't it odd, that one would not notice an extreme intelligence behind the design of such perfectly relevant markers showing up on time? A mere physical system of "magnetics" such as LOA proposes, would have much more randomness in it. You just don't know when the attracting thoughts and feelings are going to grab on to the desired elements that compose the desired outcome! The fact that there *is* so much waiting around for answers shows that the whole magnetics paradigm is an impersonal system that is inefficient. But wait! Neither can people of faith say that waiting on God for answers to prayer is any more quick and efficient even if it is more personal. Unfortunately, nobody has "the secret" on making Time flow the way we want.

LOA theorists advise us to deliberately *not* think about our problems while we are attracting solutions. Distraction is the key technique in this approach. The distraction is to think about something more pleasant, something that you want to see happen, while you are waiting around for good news. The missing piece in this little program, is WHERE you have sent your request. The metaphysical ether? Your intention has to interact with something, since we are invoking physics in LOA. In terms of feeling any satisfaction, how can "the universe" be of any comfort? Rather, this author would vote to be heard by a Someone who is aware, thinking, compassionate, and able to act. Yet we imagine this Being to be very busy; so where do we put our worries and requests? Many images have been offered for where to "put" problems: at the foot of heaven's throne, at the foot of the cross, in the hands of the Almighty, into a basket or a box, throwing them over the fence, tossing them off a bridge, cooking them in a stewpot, or sprinkling them out into the Milky Way. The point is to choose an image that carries feelings for you, as a vehicle. Once you have decided where to put this emotional content, then it makes sense to move on to the distract-and-replace stage of Waiting Around.

If someone you care about is going through an ordeal, or needs an answer to a problem, what happens? There is a lot of waiting around. People keep asking "Has anything happened yet?" The person living through the difficulty asks themselves, "Why hasn't anything happened yet?" This is most annoying. A toddler in this situation would be crying just out of pure frustration but adults can't quite bring themselves to do this. What to do instead? A little distraction goes a long way. If your imagination is tired from too much LOA visualizing, of how the future will look, perhaps it is time to borrow a reading from an inspiring text:

> One day a man from Baal-shalishah brought the man of God [Elisha] a sack of fresh grain and twenty loaves of barley bread made from the first grain of his harvest. Elisha said, "Give it to the group of prophets so they can eat." "What?" his servant exclaimed. "Feed only one hundred people with this?" But Elisha repeated, "Give it to the group of prophets so they can eat, for the Lord says there will be plenty for all. There will even be some left over!" He set it before them, they ate, and had some left, according to the word of the Lord. (2 Kings 4:42-44)

This story helps us feel good. Perhaps we will get to participate and receive such blessings. It sets up an appealing rhythm or "flow" of events. Let's compare this with the way LOA theory talks about energy flow. LOA theory makes a bet on the energy that comes from appetites or desires. The assumption is that, if a person's interest can be summoned, then so can the motivation to go after that desire. We have to give LOA theory credit for jump-starting those who are suffering from apathy. Many people say that they just don't care about anything and are not motivated to do anything in particular. A person suffering from apathy needs to get the juices flowing while avoiding the trap of jealousy when they activate their list of desires. Perhaps they were avoiding caring about anything because of the low self-esteem that comes when comparing one's self to what other people have going on. This is why it is so important to stay on the side of appreciating, and not slip over into longing or craving.

Staying on the side of appreciating one's own dreams means staying focused on feeling the good outcomes of the story or the sequence of events that have already been laid down in one's mind. LOA is good at reminding us to be consistent in our daily practice, just like an athlete in training.

6   IS ENERGY THE SAME AS MOOD?

Our next question is: How energetic is the state of Appreciation? Is it mellow or is it bubbly? It seems that there are both kinds. Perhaps the difference is how much the weight of blame is covering over the appreciation. Let's hypothesize that I am appreciating you in a mellow way. I can see many, many of your good qualities, but I can also see your shortcomings too. So I am leaning only slightly away from "neutral." It would be easy for a flicker of blame to cross my mind and alter my perceptions of you. Next, let us raise the level of energy up to bubbly. I am deliberately appreciating you for all of your strengths and I am looking intently for your good qualities (like a nurturing parent or spouse would do). Also, feeling good, I am assuming that you like me in return. This boosts the energy again. Next, if I surmise that your presence is really good for me, then the energy goes up another notch. If you agree that you like being with me too, then it is truly a good idea to spend time together, because we feel lucky to know each other. That is a very high level of energy. Blame is far in the background at this point. The blessings are getting a free rein to propagate. Naturally, the mood is good when friends like this gather and beneficial things happen.

LOA writers talk about deliberate co-creation as if such patterns of giving and receiving have not been around for thousands of years. To put this in simple terms, setting up an energy system of Blessings was the exact reason Christ needed to show up in Palestine during the Roman occupation. It was as if there were no good feelings left within a 500-mile radius! He had to start a new chain of good feelings so that others could get the idea to reciprocate. Imagine how the Roman military presence must have made even people from the same ethnic group suspicious of trusting or helping each other! Fear had a grip on the entire culture. Even the Roman bureaucrats hated being stuck in such a backwater place. They did not want to be there, even if they were in charge of things. The locals blamed the government, and the government blamed the locals for being hard to govern.

Avoiding the negative energy of blame is very difficult to do. We see it first and foremost in global and national politics. Since very few people are satisfied with the way legislation or elections turn out, the tendency is for avoidance of that whole aspect of life. They have 'checked out' just to protect themselves from frustration. Perhaps this is also why so many people choose to live alone. They cannot figure out how to share life with someone else without falling into the tempting trap of the blame game. This is also true at the office, where people often prefer to work alone so that they do not have to be critical of others, nor be criticized by them. It is astonishing to see how quickly a relationship or a working group can descend into such negativity. We have all felt the emotional temperature of a situation drop to sub-zero. It almost seems suffocating, as if there is no way to breathe except to escape for air. What does that tell you about the energy associated with moods?

At this point in the cycle of mood changes there would be a desperate need for an energy boost toward Acceptance. This is probably why we see so much about Tolerance in media campaigns to end prejudice against alternative lifestyles or minority groups. Acceptance is the first step, energetically speaking, and one notch above neutral. But why stop there? If everyone is really hoping for Abundance, keep going and push through from Acceptance to genuine Affinity then on to Blessing. Enough blessings in a row make a person feel that beautiful flow of basking in Abundance. The relationship can turn around. Political parties can share power. Culturally oppressed people can have a voice and some self-respect.

The LOA theorists are very wise to get us to notice the intentions that those around us are projecting. Is the other person in the room with you attracting goodness or darkness, or perhaps a mix that comes across as neutral? LOA teaches us to emphasize ways to connect positively with the good in each person in our office, club, or church; whether this goodness is on display (obvious) or not. Next, moving over to the family, parents who are trying to raise positive, healthy children have a beautiful bond of attraction with them, which hopefully (and according to design) sustains the family for many decades. When we notice the teenage years, the moodiness of adolescence comes across as a mix of light and dark, positive and negative. Yet often their intentions are to be cool (or more adult) as they move away from childhood. These transitioning years can mean that the shadows of low mood creep in, especially while there are worries about peer groups and self-esteem. This leads to our next chapter about what to do when other people in your family are dragging you down with their low moods.

7 WHEN OTHERS DRAG US DOWN

The hardest thing about family life is the necessity for going to the family for comfort when the person you have chosen (any given family member) is not prepared to give comfort at that moment in time. So what does one do when comfort is desired or needed, and no one is available to give this?

The LOA writers would tell you that each one of us is responsible for our own positive feelings. The positive feelings are ready and available because of "staying open to the Source." Put another way, if a person has been working at building up positive thinking habits in their mind, such as practicing affirmations, then good feelings should be available to tap into on demand. This kind of technique of "flipping over into good feelings" during a difficult situation is unique to LOA. Before LOA became popular, cognitive-behavioral theory techniques (CBT) were, and still are, used to cultivate a comforting series of thoughts among the din of riotous self-criticism or blaming others. Comforting thoughts are easier to reach for than outright enthusiasm, especially if your favorite daydreams are remote from daily life (like your favorite vacation spot). When you are feeling oppressed by a harsh reality, which of these two thoughts feels better: "it's okay just for today, because nothing changes over night" versus the more expansive thought "I see myself smiling in the sunshine while hiking on a cliff overlooking the ocean"? The first one is a small step from your troubles, the second one is farther away (from your current state) but packs more punch to get you off the ground. The more you have practiced positive states, it will not be so hard to convince yourself to access such an ideal scene quickly.

It takes training to reach within oneself and find stability. It takes even more training to feel jazzed up "no matter what." But this is exactly what the LOA is attempting. It takes training in the spiritual life so that one feels confident that when the going gets tough, the assurance will be there from God, while looking to scripture or spiritual classics for inspiration. Sometimes reading guidance in a book still falls flat. Then we need another person who believes as we do, to persuade us to feel safe again. Thus, I would add that a community of faith needs to be on the "go to" list of how to get "re-connected to the Source." Other positive people, who have weathered difficult times, can give you a boost on a day when you just cannot lift yourself up to the level of good feelings.

The Holy Spirit speaks through other people to you. Similarly, you may feel inspired to say a kind word of encouragement to others who are suffering from a low mood. The only gray area here is how much and how often you end up needing other people to help you. It might be useful to observe yourself. How needy are you? Some neediness can connect us to our families and communities. Much neediness can de-stabilize daily functioning. The more often your own positive practice can sustain you, the better. You will be less needy. What do I mean by positive practice? Deliberately choosing to practice positive thoughts and feelings (internal) no matter what the circumstances (external). Yes, it is a dispute over which will dominate, the internal or the external. We want the inner person, the self to win against crushing misfortune. Cognitive-Behavioral techniques also do this by having you take your current feeling/thought state and reframe by increments. Think of these two methods like the difference between the speed of sound and the speed of light. Some people prefer slower and steadier.

Let's return to the subject of being needy, and talk about babies for a moment. Babies are both needy and fussy, similar to primitive emotions in adults. Besides offering comfort to the fussy baby, the other tried-and-true technique is Distraction. One thing to notice about LOA writers is that they use distraction quite well. They use it as a weapon against negativity. LOA accuses humanity of the tendency to flip or catapult into negativity. Psychological research agrees that this is one of the most predictable habits known to civilization. Right they are. So how can we distract the mind from its wily ways? First of all, what if a person is too tired to be positive? It is well known that the more drained a person gets, their resiliency goes down. The analogy is similar to asking a baby to smile too many times for the photographer at the portrait studio. Every little shiny bauble has been waved in front of the baby, every little cute sound has been tried so that baby will look over one more time and smile. At this point of saturation, the mind, like the baby, just needs a rest from all the positivity. So we stop the distractions and leave baby "as is" for awhile.

Call it contemplation or zen or listening to God, but just realize that co-creating activities, as advocated by LOA, sometimes have to be let go of for the time-being. This is similar to explaining to an extravert why an introvert needs to be alone for an hour to reset their inward sense of balance. LOA can feel very aggressive, like an out-of-control extrovert.

8 INNER LIFE

So while "co-creating" is suspended a few times a day for rest and contemplation, let's also be clear not to crowd this precious time with anything else, even practicing gratitude. LOA is always harping on gratitude exercises without consideration that this still invokes mental and verbal lists of what we are thankful for. This is a type of up-and-out verbal energy. Mindful appreciating fits more with resting because it allows just one or two ideas to be gently noticed as they spontaneously arise during that quiet hour. The way these would spontaneously arise would be for the person meditating to simply ask to be shown the abundance or the blessing of that day so far, then wait for the answer.

If one has been using the law of attraction (LOA) most of the day, then there should be no problem with anxious or melancholy thoughts intruding into contemplative or quiet times. In this regard, LOA is a friend to prayer life. People who are habitually in deep prayer, for instance in cloistered religious life, are also prone to introversion, which in turn, can lead to melancholy. Thus, the bright and sunny extroverted mindset of LOA is a perfect tonic or balancing element to the very quiet and inward life of a nun, a monk, or someone who meditates often.

So, as we are careful not to let the LOA teachings crowd out our precious moments of resting in God, we also appreciate how muscular the techniques are when we are ready to get back out in the world. There are plenty of negative situations and people in bad moods to ruin any well-crafted solace that came from a good meditation. Again, LOA techniques will be useful in preserving inner equilibrium while we handle the "downers" that come our way. If your inner equilibrium can be sustained by the two techniques of meditating and positive psychology, then the goal of this book will be met.

It has been said, critically, that people use religion as a shield, in order to keep away things that are unfamiliar to them, as well as things that are offensive. Let's be honest about defenses. Every person on this planet defends themselves against intrusions to their personality or beliefs or peace of mind. It only becomes a serious problem when a person is so over-defended that they cannot move freely through society or daily life. Interestingly, the LOA writers constantly emphasize the word "open" as in - staying open to abundance and open to change. They talk about keeping one's soul (or valve) open so that energy can flow in from the universe. This sounds like Christian writers who talk about staying open to God's love for each of us. However, love is much more personal than energy and God is much more intelligent than bits of rock and ice floating through space. What does the word Universe mean to you?

The main difference between Christian spirituality writers and LOA writers is that the latter make reference to how each person can help heal the planet by flowing healing back to troubled areas of the world. LOA theory is quite robust about personal power. The idea that each person can "co-create" new and better circumstances for our world just by exuding positive energy helps in handling sadness and anxiety over the unhealthy state of the global environment or global politics. A positive Christian would certainly pray for these things, but would expect God Almighty to put the power into getting the results. So the question is: does LOA make its followers/practitioners unnecessarily tired? If you thought the fate of the world depended on your output of positive energy all the time, would you ever let yourself rest, given the circumstances you read in the news? Probably not. Therefore, I submit to the reader that positive Christianity is more sustainable in every-day practice.

This argument I will call the argument from sustainability. That which makes you healthier is more true than that which makes you less healthy or wears you out. To be more at peace makes you more healthy. Which of these paths puts you into more balance? They are both beautiful in their positive views of the world. They both create beauty within the personhood of those who practice their techniques. Yet one has the potential to nourish the soul even more. The soul who also has the Creator as an advocate is a soul more likely to flourish. An advocate is a person not a thing, not a force of nature.

Only you will know which one of these two strengthens you the most: LOA theory or positive Christianity. They can certainly be used in tandem, on a practical level. On a philosophical level, they are in essence very different.

9 WITHERED TREES: CURSING AND FORGIVENESS

> In the morning, as they were passing, they saw the fig tree withered
> away to its roots. And Simon remembered and said to him, Master behold
> The fig tree which you cursed has withered. Jesus answered, saying to
> them, "If you have faith in God, truly I say to you, whoever should say to
> this mountain, 'Be moved and fall into the sea', and does not doubt in
> his heart, but believes that what he says will be done, it will be done to
> him. Therefore I say to you, anything you ask for in prayer, believe that
> you have received it, and it will be done for you." (Mark 11:20-24)

Before we talk about the powerful message of this verse; we must first be
fair and notice that Jesus spends the next few paragraphs talking about
forgiveness. Seemingly, this is because he didn't want his followers going
around cursing other people, just because they would have the power (after
Pentecost) to hurt, or wither, their fellow humans. Thus, the point of the
parable is **power**, just like the LOA theory is about power. However,
Christianity is going the full distance as a philosophy and including the
opposite use of power too. Jesus is demonstrating the "law of rejection"
when he curses the fig tree, in front of his disciples. A simple act of rejection
would just be a turning away, such as we do when we ignore someone
distasteful at a party. An actual cursing is the unleashing of the opposite
power of attraction. The question is: can only special beings such as Jesus do
this, or can anyone?

By the way, later in the Gospel of Mark, the fig tree is in bloom again.
Healing takes preference over cursing; yet we cannot ignore the lesson of the
withered-tree image. The usefulness of this ability to reject comes to light
when we consider a situation that calls for defending oneself. Even a
nonviolent Zen practitioner will finally rouse herself and use martial arts to
repel an attack if nothing else could be done to avert the ill intent of the
attacker. To ward off attack, the thoughts and behaviors of rejection are
invoked. Strange, but the LOA writers never admit this. They don't want to
look bad or negative. They only want to talk about being pro-active, not
defensive.

Who could blame them? Yet, it is intellectually and philosophically
dishonest not to make a place in the LOA thought-system for any rejection.
Everyone knows that to make the most of an opportunity (inherently
positive), other opportunities must be rejected. This is called "opportunity
cost." Suffering the pain of rejecting appealing choices is part of the cost. To

be fair to LOA theory, its main point is for us *not* to get into habits of rejecting or resisting everything that comes along in our daily lives.

A final observation about Jesus and the fig tree is that we can notice he did not actually chop down the fig tree. That would have been physical rejection (aggression). Instead, he put forth his intended image of how he wanted the tree to look, let this thought take effect, and then let the effect occur. He believed it would. He believed in his own power to affect the physical world. This is also a teaching of the LOA writers, but narcissistically they leave out God as a source of ultimate power.

Perhaps this is why LOA does not discuss what to do about extreme weather disasters, famine, war, or plague. It does not have an answer except to tell you, the individual, to keep your focus on positive outcomes and maintain high energy through generating good feelings. LOA theory is sensitized to the risk of humans creating more problems than they already have, just by cursing every annoying person or organization that gets in their way. Why would we want to wither our own neighborhoods, environment, workplace or elections? This story begs the question of whether we feel sorry for the fig tree. Do you? Do you enjoy cursing the world around you?

Negative Christianity is that aspect of the faith tradition that displays anger when anger could have been avoided. Many times it is in the name of, or under the guise of, being righteous and indignant. Yet if a reporter were to ask the general public what turns them off about Christianity, the most common answer would be "they are such Haters." Why do we Christians have such a reputation? The majority of Christians profess a doctrine of love and forgiveness. The main message is that God is merciful to those who turn toward Heaven and seek salvation from their misery.

Perhaps the "misery-index" of our times is indeed rising to the point that followers of Jesus Christ can't help but notice and complain. The anger seems to be about an erosion of values and a lack of wholesome choices for families and for children. The anger and the fear that parents experience in trying to raise their children the right way in 21st century America are obvious. But does raw anger help? Does it bring about solutions? Only if it is acted upon in ways that are organized and well-thought out. In other words, raw emotion has to be tempered with thought and perspective, or it will pollute the social climate that we live in. Intention must be fueled by positive thoughts and feelings about the desired outcome. Thus the message from Christ was "believe as if you have received."

10 SPEAKING OF GOD'S REPUTATION

It is astounding how much LOA writings discuss each person's ability to receive Guidance with a capital "G" and yet, at the same time, avoid discussing the existence of God. They might as well say, "May the Force be with you," as if borrowing from Taoism like Star Wars, the movie, did. (1977, Lucas) Perhaps that is where the fascination with the law of attraction came from.

If 21st century people have learned "the secret" of deliberate co-creating from hugely popular movies like *The Secret* (2006, Byrne) all the better for our planet; but why leave out God? The "secret" is a formula that is only 50% complete. To be sure, it is an inspirational exercise that impresses thousands of people, yet why doesn't this awaken our curiosity to ask for the rest of the answer? An empirically trained person would notice that something is missing in the LOA. Let's start with looking for where the motivation to even dabble with the LOA might come from. It is a remedy for apathy. People who are depressed complain that they just can't seem to be inspired about anything. LOA writings offer a way back to enthusiasm. However, for enthusiasm to have substance, it must be more than just enthusiasm for enthusiasm's sake. Into this vacancy let us put God's living Spirit, who was placed on earth for our comfort, after Christ left.

A big assumption in LOA writings is that we all need to get more in touch with our passionate dreams for a fulfilling life - so that we can gain the energy that comes from imagining how great it **will feel** to live out these dreams in reality. We have already talked about how to stay on the side of enjoyment of this process, and to stay away from feelings of jealousy or lack while we look at concrete examples of other people who have 'made it' and are living their dreams now. If you can't find any hope or dreams to get in touch with, ask for God to show you.

A person can indeed learn to regulate her/himself emotionally, using Positive Psychology techniques, but that does not mean there is no more need for a God who can offer inspiration and assistance. The Spiritual Classics are filled with highly evolved observations about how joy comes to those who wait for God to show up in small ways. God has not disappointed these seekers.

Also in LOA theory, the next point it teaches that is not quite true is the accusation that the Judaeo-Christian traditions are biased against unconventional thinking. This is patently not true. Let us consider whether having big dreams for one's life is going against the divine right order of the universe. For the record, having vision is very important in religious history. For example, from biblical writings, we have "where there is no vision, the people perish" (Proverbs 29:18). The Jewish version actually says: "Without a prophetic vision, the people throw off all restraint; but he who keeps Torah is happy." Encouraging followers of the Jewish faith to view the future as a time of wide-open possibility was not only acceptable, it was expected. Prophets, especially, were supposed to withdraw into prayer and pay close attention to their inner leadings because God communicated special privileges and tasks that way.

We cannot leave this topic without saying there is one more layer to this. The final nuance is that there is a set of priorities regarding what makes one happiest. Material abundance is not given first place on the satisfaction scale in the religious traditions. The first letter of John stipulates: "the world and its desire is passing away, but those who do the will of God live forever," (1 John 2:17). Visible signs of wealth are given primacy of place in LOA writings, because proof is needed that the techniques work. Teachings on faith have a deep concern with fulfillment on a long-term scale. When Jesus said; "I have come that they may have life, and have it abundantly," (John 10:10), he was talking about soul-satisfaction and the big picture over a life-span. We get at that issue when we ask the common funeral question, "What did this person turn into or do with their life?" **Integrity** is the main theme and hallmark of a religious viewpoint. For LOA teachings, the question would be: "How well did this person learn to attract success?" It is as if there is no other proof of the pudding. To be honest about life, it is fair to say that we each know of people who did everything they could to attract success, but the "pudding" they were in wouldn't allow it to come to pass. At least they had integrity.

Truthfully, most of us want both integrity and success, with the added assumption that integrity will lead to success. Churches and synagogues are very complimentary when one of their own can make large contributions. They are also very interested in the health and well-being of families. This is why people of faith get interested in a deliberate path to success. It is necessary to enhance the journey of faith with extra teachings about success, in order to provide materially. For this, we can be grateful to the writers who explain the LOA for purposes of economic survival and resilience.

Getting back to John's letter in the New Testament, you may ask: What is this mysterious "will of God" that he is talking about? Let's put it in distinct contrast to LOA writings. The desire that pulls you higher and farther along in your unfolding potential is the desire to discover evidence that God is alive and active here on earth. Along with this search comes the next desire, to be close to God, to be known by God, to love God and be loved by God. What does that feel like? It feels like grace – which feels like a kiss from beyond the visible plane. It feels like you are being watched very lovingly. It feels like someone important takes notice when you do something right. Also, there will be moments when you feel answered by an event in the physical world, perhaps after asking if God noticed your feelings or your difficult situation.

LOA writings hammer on the point that you must learn to love life and love the excitement of 'flowing energy' but never is the love of God mentioned. They will talk about receiving Guidance with a capital "G" yet at the same time, skirt all around describing God as aware, alive, or loving. Supposedly, the universe operates on its own and all the LOA theorists want to do is help you notice the patterns of cause and effect.

For the purposes of keeping each of us fully exercising our own free will, let's assume that it is important for us to believe in our own efficacy. This is very psychologically sound. Just because it is good for us to invoke self-determination does not make it the entire truth about what is taking place in the universe. We can see all kinds of elements and influences at work in the world outside of our individual selves. How do we know what is of God and what is not of God? How do we discover that little thread of God's possible activity during an ordinary day? It is like a Native American with her/ his ear to the ground listening for hoof-beat noises. Which one of those was special? Sometimes we only know in hindsight.

Positive Christianity as a perspective attempts to connect the approach of a blessing with its arrival by looking for the pattern of events that join them. Enthusiasm about watching God at work in the world is part of the process.

11 COINCIDENCE AS VIEWED BY LOA

The closest that LOA writers come to acknowledging the power of prayer is "validation by coincidence" otherwise known as the Universe sending hints that you are on the right path. The idea is to stay enthusiastic and passionate about manifesting your intentions until something happens. This is not very different from what people of faith do when watching events in daily life to see if God is answering their prayers in small ways, or in stages of a bigger answer (long-term solution). Either way, we are talking about encouraging signs that make you feel as if "everything is going to be okay." Both systems of thought are similar in this matter.

The difference between the two ways of seeing the cosmos comes down to how much power any one person has. LOA describes a human being as a dynamic engine, releasing energy into a field of consciousness that opens up to the correctly tuned vibrations sent forth by positive feelings and thoughts. Christian cosmology, generally speaking, lines up with a definition of human personhood that prioritizes the power of the Creator over that of the individual. Yet, since the individual is loved and esteemed by God, the exercise of individual capability is encouraged. When good things happen, one could say that the individual's prerogative has been enhanced or approved of by God.

To put this in even more starkly contrasting terms, it could be said that LOA theory is a natural law theory. Miracles do not occur because God has intervened. Unusual, serendipitous events happen because the energetic human has tapped into the best possible frequency of positive brain/body functioning. LOA writers don't have an explanation as to why the universe would be programmed to assist human beings. What is the source of such fundamental helpfulness and altruism?

For faith-based practitioners of Positive Psychology, the most exciting aspect of believing in God is watching circumstances or people change for the better. True, this can take a very long time if the troubled person (the one being prayed for) cannot find much to be thankful for. Here we find concurrence with LOA observations of the way life works. It is interesting to watch a prayer group aim intentions of health and healing at a very sick person. Many circumstances will change around that person, even if they insist on remaining focused on their own pain. It is as if a very ill person cannot cooperate with their own cure. This more than anything else is proof of individual power to block out the Light, instead of receive, or even attract the Light.

LOA writers encourage you to become a creator of positive outcomes. The teaching they want to get across is that **reactive** people always lose out. Reactivity is a dynamic that starts with the person feeling pinned against the wall, or extremely fed-up with the same old nonsense. They feel powerless to control or change the situation or the people around them. It can look like aggressiveness or merely defensiveness. The point is, at the moment of reactivity, they forget their own power to influence outcomes.

The appeal of using prayer, in addition to LOA, is that when the individual self is inadequate or forgetful, it is easier to reach for the higher power of God. Not only that, but a steady habit of prayer puts a person out in front of the whole cycle of reactivity because positive influence is being exerted before the situation reaches a crisis. Prayer is somewhat like planning ahead; there is more chance that situations can turn out better.

Another difference between religious faith and LOA is that LOA assumes your motivations are good enough (to create positive outcomes). The teachings about prayer are careful to ask you to try to align your will with what you understand about God's ways, or just to say "I align my will with God's purposes." So what is the big deal about proper intent? From the Christian tradition there is an interesting point about this in Mark 11:23-26. The Holy Spirit cannot move freely if there are grudges or anger, so Jesus teaches about forgiveness in the same lesson as the moving of mountains. Great faith (or energy) is not sufficient in and of itself. Negative motivations or feelings must be reckoned with and tamed before circumstances change.

12 IT'S NOT SLEIGHT OF HAND

One of the amazing things about reading LOA theory is how much faith is placed in our ability to generate good feelings. If you read the literature on depression, you will know how hard it is for a depressed person to consistently come up with things to be happy about. This task alone can take many hours of counseling before a melancholy person even believes that there is actually goodness present in their lives. Yet LOA writers not only insist that you can generate good feelings, they also insist that good things will begin to happen more frequently the more you stay on the 'feel-good' side of your brain. Well, this is bribery! (Parents know that bribery works). The parental message to their children is "if you behave well, life at home will go better for you." The message of LOA is to get a person into the cycle of intending good things, then watching good things happen. Repeat often as needed. Is this a trick or sleight-of-hand?

Persuasion is definitely a hallmark of LOA teachings. LOA writers try very hard to convince you that this course of positive thinking will work. If you don't believe the theory, you are not going to try hard enough. A struggle ensues between the reader's resistance and the writer's powers to convince. It is just as much of an uphill slog as trying to prove why faith in God is worthwhile. But wait, we are talking about faith either way. At least when it comes to religion, there are huge numbers of people around the world who believe in God. When it comes to LOA theory, not that many people have heard of it. It is harder to argue from historical precedent. What is easy about LOA is how we want it to be true. Since it sounds too good to be true, we are held back by our doubts.

Back to the assumption that trickery is necessary. If you agree with the research that has observed a "negativity bias" in the human mind, then it will not seem untruthful or unethical that great spiritual teachers will try to talk you out of this tendency. If they cannot talk you out of your suspicions, then they will try to get you to "test-drive" or pretend to be happy until you get a feel for it. LOA is an experiment in believing good things about the universe and your role here. As much as faith-based teachers hate to admit it, having faith **is** an experimental endeavor until the person gets comfortable with it. I would like to thank LOA authors for demonstrating this process to the rest of the world. The simplicity of it is quite elegant: intend to be happy, then watch happiness grow. Meanwhile, ignore your negativity bias. Name that negativity as the raven that it is, ready to peck away at your peace of mind.

I would also like to thank LOA theory for pointing out another feature of how faith works. The LOA writers want you to notice how positive thoughts and intentions create an energy field of safety around the participant. The idea behind this is still based on the paradigm of the "energy-flow" of emotions - which attract order and health to the person in their daily circumstances. In other words, a cloak or a shirt is getting sewn together to wrap the person in positive awareness (images, thoughts, and feelings). For those readers who have studied martial arts, this idea is similar to building up 'chi' energy, and wrapping the body in it for enhanced performance. LOA is similar to "Iron Shirt" technique for the body, except it is for the mind.

Any person reading this book knows that one of the many things that religion has to offer is protection. Prayers are for requesting protection (from harm or from evil). Watching prayers get answered motivates believers to keep praying and even encourages skeptics to try asking for protection in the same way. So what can be said to a person who tried prayer and didn't receive the help they asked for? Thanks to the LOA theory, we can now look more carefully at what is put into the prayer. It never hurts to raise one's level of prayer to a new level of maturity. LOA writers would have us look carefully to make sure we are **not** contributing to our own problems. This is a "take responsibility for yourself" principle. If a person is ill, it is very important to avoid imagining themselves as ill when they pray for help. This carefulness is more for the subconscious mind than it is about any rules God has about how to correctly visualize the prayer. Most of the religious teachings about how to pray are more about having the proper respect and humility when approaching the One who is Holy.

Let's say a person is trying to take responsibility for how s/he prays. Let's also assume that this person is already physically ill, but they have a cheerful spirit about it and keep trying to stay on the side of optimism. They have high hopes for recovery. There is still time for this person to influence the outcome. Naturally, receiving encouragement from well-meaning friends and family will tip the advantage toward health even more. By contrast, if we are talking about a person who is very sick, to the point of not having emotional or psychological strength left to practice affirmations or prayers; then the probability is toward a downward spiral. They will get worse and worse because it is hard for them to imagine or believe that it is possible to heal. Worse, they may begin to believe it is their fate to remain ill. Interestingly, LOA writers call this state of a very sick person, "too cut off from their source."

This sounds like a personal source because the focus of LOA writings is on the resources of the individual. A theologically minded person will tell you that God has many ways to break into a person's self-made prison. The very least that the ill person can do is be open to and accepting of the compassion and strength offered by acquaintances and relatives. This is important to remember because the tendency of a very sick person is to resist, resist, resist! Resisting help and resisting change is a recipe for not only being stuck, but for heading straight to extinction. One exception must be noted: a terminally-ill person, going through the process of dying, will shut down naturally without there being any way for caregivers to stop it. There is no shame in this type of letting go and giving up.

The caregivers can still offer optimism about where the dying person is going after this life (as long as there is an expressed belief in heaven on the part of the dying person).

Another philosophical or theological mistake that LOA writers make would be their pantheism. This is easy to correct, but it sounds something like this: "the universe is benevolent and intends good for you." Why are we purposefully ignoring or misnaming all the bone-crunching possibilities out there? The universe is a mixture of injury and kindness. To be sure, we can probably agree that human experience shifts according to what each particular person has been focusing upon. LOA writers are like coaches trying to get each individual to stay focused on a "well-being zone," or a healthy mindset. But to equate all of reality with *only* what happens when one is in "the well-being zone" is not truthful. It would be more accurate to say "when a person is in the well-being zone and can stay there consistently, then the universe will eventually cooperate." However, a double-bind is set up; reader beware! You have to stay calm, centered, and grateful OR ELSE bad things will happen. How does that threat make you feel? Inspired or tired? If it makes you tired, that is a hint that it is not working for you.

One of the most beautiful verses for a weary person to hear when they need more inspiration, comes from the Christian tradition. It is from a letter that Paul wrote to the Romans (Chapter 8):

> Likewise the Spirit helps us in our weakness; for we do not know how to pray
> as we ought, but that very Spirit intercedes with sighs too deep for words. And
> God, who searches the heart, knows what is the mind of the Spirit, because
> the Spirit intercedes for the saints according to the will of God. (vs. 26-28)

It is not necessarily up to us to say our prayers correctly, or have the proper attitude (but it helps). This teaching offers mercy and rest. The Holy Spirit is stronger than one little mind pitted against the forces of the universe, and also against all the horrible things that can go wrong. If all I had was the Law of Attraction, I would be afraid. Afraid to misuse it, get it wrong, not practice enough, not have enough appreciation, not have enough enthusiasm, and get blamed for carrying around just a little too much negativity, so that when something went wrong, it was my own fault for being over the limit allowable.

So please do practice the LOA, but remember who has your back when you are down and cannot swing the bat or wear the iron shirt of Positive Psychology.

13 IN THE LONG RUN

By far, the greatest contribution that LOA provides to the larger field of Positive Psychology is its heightened understanding of inspiration/spontaneity: meaning "catching" the moment's fresh idea and riding it for all the juice contained therein. This method excels in looking for the good in everything. It is also has a very hearty dose of motivation for why a person should keep trying in the face of neutral or poor results. Furthermore, LOA theory gives a reason why covetousness or envy does not have to play a role in enjoying a daydream or visualization. For example, let's say you have always wanted a horse but didn't get one. Now that you have grown out of childhood, it is likely that you are saying "I'll never have a horse." Tomorrow, when you see a beautiful brand-new horse trailer cruising down the highway, containing two well-groomed horses, how will you handle the moment?

Classical religious teaching would have you thinking "I shall not covet what is my neighbor's property." If you are a practitioner of LOA, you will borrow that happy thought of a beautiful horse for several minutes. The happy thought will lead to many pleasurable feelings of past enjoyment, then you will send it out asking for good things to happen, saying "If it can happen for them, it can happen for me. I receive this gift in the future." You have now opened yourself up to a happier day and a happier future, even if you don't know the outcome of your wish. You have borrowed a positive "updraft" from the visual world around you. If you look at it as a free experiential gift, then you will feel lucky for a few hours. As you know from other Positive Psychology writings, the finesse of this little practice is to emphasize the gratitude and minimize the sense of lack.

This technique will work over and over again, all day long, if you just stay away from feeling entitled or deprived. What do I mean by entitlement? Entitlement is the thought that you deserve something more than other people, due to your superiority. Isn't it amazing when we meet someone who acts entitled? They have been blessed with something, or many things, that we all want and yet somehow they believe it is due to some intrinsic merit they have, that other people do not have. Sometimes they will call it 'savvy' or a higher I.Q., or being well-bred or luck or God's favor. None of this is true. Why? It could fall away at any time. God could decide to answer one prayer instead of another. The privilege could be given to someone else. Another person's horse could be given to you.

LOA writers will tell you that it is only your daily "attracting" that is building up the emotional reservoir needed to keep these goodies from disappearing. Is this true? From a philosophical point of view, there is no way to know 'The Formula' that keeps misfortune away. The faults and merits of any system can be debated. From a psychological point of view, we know from research, that thoughts and beliefs which make us feel better on a daily basis also help keep us optimistic, incrementally over time. This in turn lends itself to behaviors which increase success and better outcomes, such as: not giving up on opportunities or secondary options. So here we have the case of a principle which is relevant psychologically, but not provable philosophically, unless we admit psychological data as proof.

Religious writers will *not* promise that you can keep misfortune at bay. They know better. They also know better than to try and explain what God is or is not doing in a particular situation. Also, a religious writer would focus on the need for each person to be humble when speaking to God about receiving help. LOA writers are much more bold in advising us to "take the bull by the horns" and sculpt/conjure up a bright future NO MATTER WHAT. It is this insistence on the right to feel good that is so unique to LOA theory. It is radical and adamant.

This leaves us with the question: is humility a key ingredient? Upon the answer hangs your choice of the best fit between you and these two worldviews; (1) Positive Christianity, or (2) LOA teachings. As you ponder your choice, here is a quote from former President Jimmy Carter:

> *I have never been disappointed when I asked in a humble and sincere way for God's help. I pray often. I think I pray more often since January 12th.* [When he became the governor of the state of Georgia in 1971]

14 THE HILARIOUS LIFE OF LOA IMAGERY

One of the benefits of borrowing tips from LOA technique is that your prayer life gets much more interesting. Think of it as similar to Art Therapy or Play Therapy in your head. The essential thing here is to put a visual structure on top of your thoughts so that they are more enhanced than words alone. This also amps up the feelings by one notch.

If you still can't grasp what the point is, let's take an example from the world of mental health settings. Imagine a clinic with a child or a teen walking into a room filled with an overflowing abundance of symbolic figures: statues and toys and building pieces. The person then chooses some of these to express ideas and feelings while explaining an imaginary story, or something that actually happened (or a mix of the two). The amazing thing about this endeavor is that bucketfuls of meaning are wrapped up in the symbolic objects that are chosen during this timeframe (50 minutes). Also, good feelings result when the most cheerful objects are chosen.

Back to prayer: let's say that you are trying to pray in a more positive way than you used to pray. Previously, you asked God to "bless my friends and my family and don't let anything bad happen." There is not much emotional or visceral zing to such a quick phrase. It is mostly verbal and rational, yet the intentions are still good. To add some LOA clout to this type of prayer, the energy of good feelings would need to be deliberately invoked. Remember how your music teacher used to say "Play it again, except with more feeling"? So what could we pull off the shelves of an Art/Play Therapy room to get going with this? Here are a few objects to visualize: a shiny star of destiny, a fountain with birds, a bright colorful rainbow, glitter to throw around, sparkling red hearts, a powerful bird with outspread wings, a sword, a knight on horseback, a shield, an airplane, a speed boat, or a big green shamrock. For money, just thinking of the words bank account in a digital way has no visual/emotional pull compared to concrete images of gold coins, green bills, and shiny stones that represent rubies, emeralds, amethyst, sapphires, and diamonds. You get the idea about fun images pulling positive feeling.

To make these images work in an "affective" prayer, imagine spreading the rainbow over your family member who is hurting, while they smile at *all* the colors. The friend who needs a job gets a shining star of fame and attention over their head, along with the prayer for them to receive money. The co-worker who is sad receives an image of you passing a red heart of comfort and compassion into the palm of their hand. The point is that more of your energy is released into the prayer because it more than just abstract thought. The images are a bridge to the feelings.

If you are praying for a lonely person but you don't want to layer over their sadness with more images of loneliness, then you might imagine a gurgling fountain in a garden where they are sitting watching the birds splash and chirp. You are praying for them to be able to see the beauty in nature and receive healing from the goodness of it, with rays of sunshine from heaven falling around their shoulders. You can also picture a circle of new friends surrounding them.

In terms of praying for strength, you can picture a huge eagle flying over the person's head, looking down on them like the eye of God. For a person who is in danger, such as a teenager at a large school with gangs, your prayer can be of a large shield over and around the person while you pray for protection for them. This is one reason why the image of St. Michael the Archangel is so popular.

If you are worried about war breaking out somewhere around the globe, you can visualize a dove of peace with an olive branch flying over each country several times, reminding them of the great value of peace and diplomatic negotiations between countries. If you need a poetic verse to reinforce the image, then you can borrow this from a statue at the United Nations. It is a quote from the Jewish prophet Isaiah (chapter 2), also found in Micah (chapter 4): "nation shall not lift up sword against nation, neither shall they learn war any more; but they shall sit under their own fig trees, and no one shall make them afraid; for the mouth of the Lord of hosts has spoken."

These images utilize more of your mind/awareness than just thinking words and thoughts. Also, the best that LOA technique has to offer us is how to help manifest what we *do* want and not reinforce what we don't want. If only each newspaper article could have a sidebar about what to do with the sad news of another massacre, instead of just dumping the bad feelings on the readers and assuming they will figure out how to handle such depressing news! No wonder citizens don't want to stay informed. But now you have the tool of positive imagery when you pray about world events. Please contribute your best hopes.

15 EVEN THOUGH IT HELPS

So far we have been looking at the merits of both systems of belief: Law of Attraction teachings and Christian wisdom. The main difference is how they each handle negative feelings. LOA theory just wants each person to stay away from Negativity. In this sense, it is purist in its approach. One might even call it an aesthetic principle, which means that Perfection of feeling is its highest goal. Therein rests its greatest difficulty: such perfection discourages many who would otherwise join the fan club. If the bar is set too high, many people won't even try. But for those who love a challenge, nothing short of Perfection will gain any respect.

As for Christianity, perfection of feelings is not a primary goal; yet among mature Christians it is a highly sought-after state of being. The example set by Jesus is one of recognizing difficult feelings while at the same time offering peace. For instance in the story called "The hemorrhaging woman" (Mark 5:25 – 34), we find a person who is following Jesus around and imagining/believing that she will be well again if she can just touch the cloak of the famous healer. Events unfolded just as she had hoped. Still, she was afraid to admit that she was the one who had snuck in close to touch his cloak. Remember that he requested to know who had received the healing. When Jesus said "your faith has healed you…" this would not have surprised a follower of the Law of Attraction because the woman had set up the conditions (in her mind) to receive an improvement. A Christian would notice the fact that she had been suffering for 12 years and had not been helped by any doctors (vs. 26). Also, a faith-based observer would marvel that only the Savior, the Christ could resolve those 12 years of searching and hoping.

So it comes down to this predicament: is the sick person responsible for holding themselves back from healing (partially or completely)? LOA theory says the person is completely responsible for their own experience of pulling away from illness. Christianity teaches that God does one part, the faithful person does the other part, by obeying God's laws and invoking faith. Lest anyone say that God does it all, just look around at all the examples of religiously oriented people who **stay sick** and are miserably depressed about their whole situation; versus those religiously oriented people who do improve because they have had a positive outlook in addition to their faith in God. The hemorrhaging woman took 12 years to get it right, as viewed through the lens of LOA teachings. A Christian would say that Jesus' earthly ministry only lasted three years, and she had to wait for the Master to show up. Also, a Christian view of this situation would admit that suffering happens regardless, unlike LOA theory which tries to brush suffering under the rug by calling it poor technique. If proper technique were used, suffering would not happen, according to the advocates of LOA.

For the record, let's talk about why Christianity does tolerate suffering without trying to explain it away. Historically, the justification for respecting suffering is the moral lesson that we learn from it, in measured doses. But to get stuck in suffering, with no way back to normal life, is what most of us, religious or non-religious, want to avoid. Yet we can't forget those extreme ascetics who gain deep meaning by offering up their suffering for the purification of a sinful world or for the benefit of loved ones. For an example of a radical view of suffering, look at the writings of St. Therese of Lisieux. This person's life is a very complicated mix of LOA and pain. She believed it was beneficial for her to suffer physical agony in order to attract God's grace and God's attention.

Speaking of those who prefer to be a bit more serious or melancholy, it should be noted that in a faith-based approach to life, you don't have to be perfectly positive and "flowing energy" correctly every hour of the day in order to get what you need, or even want, **but it helps**. What helps? To aim for the sacred joy of heaven as much as possible. This joy is available and accessible and it is just as positive and energetic as the high octane good feelings that LOA writers spend so much time describing. Thank you to the LOA writers for describing the non-religious version of these wonderful feelings. It has helped us all try harder to get there.

Practitioners of LOA dream big, then imagine the dreams coming true, then repeat over and over until they are achieved. They also add in "scripting" which is a form of journal-writing about all the good outcomes hoped for. The power of the subconscious mind is invoked again and again. This is all very well and good except - when it doesn't work. Why does it sometimes fail? A Christian theologian would add a careful stipulation here. Notice the exception found in the New Testament Epistle of James. The fine print reads like this: "You ask and you do not receive because you ask wrongly, you ask so that you may satisfy your lusts." (James 4:3) Thus, the formula does not work if the person has insincere intentions. Sorting out who has worthy enough goals is so tricky that LOA writers don't seem to touch it. Only God can do that. Perhaps LOA writers surmise that unanswered desires will be extinguished or forgotten as the person moves on to the next goal. There is always something more to set one's sights on!

Before we leave this topic of who gets their prayers answered and who doesn't, let's agree that no matter which of these practices you follow, this book was written to wish you the very best life possible. May you have a life of abundance, may you practice good feelings and gratitude, may your prayers call forth blessings, and may your optimism lift and encourage others who are down.

Margot Schultz

RELATED READING

Brother Lawrence (1977). *The practice of the presence of God.* New York: Random House.

Byrne, R. (2006). *The secret.* New York: Atria Books.

Carlson, R. (1992/1997). *You can be happy no matter what: five principles for keeping life in perspective.* Novato: New World Library.

Grabhorn, L. (2000). *Excuse me, your life is waiting: the astonishing power of feelings.* Charlottesville: Hampton Roads.

Hay, L. (1990). *Heart thoughts: a treasury of inner wisdom.* Santa Monica: Hay House.

Lewis, C.S. (1947/1974). *Miracles.* New York: HarperCollins.

Seligman, M. E. P. (2002). *Authentic happiness: using the new positive psychology to realize your potential for lasting fulfillment.* New York: Simon & Schuster.

Seligman, M. E. P. (1990/1998). *Learned optimism: how to change your mind and your life.* New York: Knopf.

Shimoff, M. (2008). *Happy for no reason: 7 steps to being happy from the inside out.* New York: Simon & Schuster.

Taylor, T. S. (2010). *The science behind the secret: decoding the law of attraction and the universal quantum connection.* Wake Forest: Baen Books.

ABOUT THE AUTHOR

Margot Schultz, M.T.S., M.A., NCC lives in the stressful culture of Washington DC and Northern Virginia. She has spent many decades trying to integrate what she has learned in her academic studies in the fields of Philosophy, Theology, and Mental Health Counseling. In addition, she has been in more book clubs than she can possibly count. Hopefully this book will contribute to some fine discussions for all readers and seekers.